SOUL AMONG LIONS

Musings of a Bootleg Preacher

WILL D. CAMPBELL

with illustrations by Jim Hsieh

Westminster John Knox Press

LOUISVILLE

LONDON · LEIDEN

Book design by Bonnie Campbell

First edition

Published by Westminster John Knox Press
Louisville, Kentucky

This book is printed on acid-free paper that meets the American
National Standards Institute Z39.48 standard. ∞

Printed in the United States of America

01 02 03 04 05 06 07 08 — 10 9 8 7 6 5 4 3

Library of Congress Cataloging-in-Publication Data
Campbell, Will D.
    Soul among lions : musings of a bootleg preacher /
Will. D. Campbell. — 1st ed.
        p.   cm.
   ISBN 0-664-22130-0 (alk. paper)
   1. Christian life—Anecdotes.   2. Campbell, Will D.—
Anecdotes. I. Title.
BV4517.C35 1999
277.3'0829—dc21   98-53718

FOR GRANDMA BERTHA AND GRANDPA BUNT,
WHO TAUGHT ME ABOUT HARD SAYINGS

I LIE DOWN AMONG LIONS
    THAT GREEDILY DEVOUR HUMAN PREY;
THEIR TEETH ARE SPEARS AND ARROWS,
    THEIR TONGUES SHARP SWORDS.

BE EXALTED, O GOD, ABOVE THE HEAVENS.
    LET YOUR GLORY BE OVER ALL THE EARTH.

PSALM 57:4–5 (NRSV)

PREFACE

SOME WHILE BACK THE PRODUCER OF THE TELEVISION SHOW *NEWS ODYSSEY* ASKED ME TO do an occasional commentary. Some of the essays in this volume were written for those telecasts. I am grateful to *News Odyssey* for asking me to do them and for granting permission for their use here.

This is, simply put, a medley of little ditties. They have no particular theme and follow no determined order or arrangement. They reflect whatever I might have been mad at, glad about, exulting in on a given day. Some of them express the chafing of an old man grown weary of what he sees as institutional nonsense. Sheer evil. Other pieces celebrate the glory of God revealed in some event or person.

They are all highly subjective, bubblings from the depths of one man's soul. A soul that for the adult years of three quarters of a century has been aroused to anger by the roaring of the lions, but also refreshed and comforted by the tenderness of little lambs. Some of the ire may be rooted in my own restless temperament, impatience with things one is expected to accept as, after all, only human. But it is my hope that the anger reflects at least a mild flirtation with the radical Christ Movement.

The fragments of compassion flow, in my mind, from an abounding joy in the miracles God hath wrought in the lives and deeds of some of his creation. Altogether they are bits and pieces from the ditty box of one follower of the Way. Albeit from afar.

WILL D. CAMPBELL

SOUL AMONG LIONS

I

STILL WE HEAR TALK OF DESPAIR OVER RACIAL DIVISIONS AND TEENAGE CRIME. THERE IS much to warrant concern, but are there not also promising signs we sometimes overlook? An incident in our rural community recently gave me hope. Two years ago our nearest neighbors, a couple from what is called the blue-collar class, experienced a grim tragedy. Their teenage grandson was murdered by his mother, who also killed herself. This past Christmas Eve, when the grandmother entered the cemetery for her weekly pilgrimage, she saw a young black male standing near the grandson's tomb. She did not recognize him. His dress and bearing would have frightened some, suggesting to them felonious intent. He held something in his hand and moved toward the woman as she approached. What he held was not an Uzi, not a Saturday night special, not a knife. It was a long-stemmed rose, shimmering in the winter's chilly mist. With a smiling greeting, he offered her the rose, and together they leaned down and placed it on the grave.

"I come here often," he said. "Matt was my best friend at school."

An elderly white woman of the yeomanry and a young black man of the urban poor, in solemn accord in a country graveyard. Mourning, loving, remembering. Together. Perplexed, but not despairing.

We shall overcome? Only in ways like that.

<hr/>

II

EVERY TWO YEARS THERE IS A NEW TERM OF CONGRESS TO PASS NEW LAWS. TROUBLE IS, the more laws there are to break, the more criminals we have. That requires more prisons. Maybe we have enough laws. If something hasn't been against the law for five hundred years, maybe we don't really need a law to prohibit it. We started out with ten commandments, and of that number, only two are still crimes. Honoring parents, graven images, adultery, keeping the Sabbath, lying, coveting our neighbor's ass—all those things have gone by the board. Except in certain political situations.

The main topics of Congress these days are welfare, crime, balancing the budget, and campaign reform. Everyone knows they aren't serious about that last one. Or about balancing the budget and welfare. How would it be if Congress didn't meet for one term? They and their staffs cost approximately six billion dollars per term. That wouldn't balance the budget, but it would help. Crime would decrease because there wouldn't be any new laws to break. And when Congress did go back to work after not having been paid for two years, maybe they would be a little more sensitive to the poor. Maybe welfare would be more humane.

III

THERE'S SOMETHING ABOUT OUR PRIORITIES. ONCE AGAIN WE'RE HEARING TALK ABOUT amending the Constitution to make burning the flag a crime. Since the Constitution was written, the average of reported flag burnings has been fewer than one per year. That doesn't strike me as being of epidemic proportions. Like, say, drive-by shootings of children, or families living on the streets. Why don't we tackle that constitutionally?

Wisdom is sometimes found in unexpected places. I heard a country song the other day that spoke to the matter of flags. It said raising the flag is the same thing as raising your voice, and, whether freak or preacher, we all have the right to be heard. The singer said you can't burn his flag because it flies in his heart and mind. It is a symbol, not a piece of cloth from an assembly line. The song ended like this:

> We'll fly that flag so high that it's out of
> your reach,
> But while we're about it, we might burn
> the freedom of speech.*

Think about it.

*From "The Flag Song" by Tom T. Hall. © Hallnote Music.

IV

I WATCH THE POLITICAL PROCESS PRETTY MUCH AS
I WATCH BASEBALL. I HAVE A FAVORITE TEAM,
but I know that ultimately it makes no difference
who wins. I gave up on politics offering any hope for
the world's problems a long time ago. It's an illusion, a
mirage. Sometimes good comedy. For example, I've been
watching the Senate hearings on campaign reform. I sat
with amused incredulity as Senator Thompson, who
happens to be my senator, began. With feigned outrage
he said his committee had reason to believe that a Chi-
nese operative had attempted to influence an election in
the United States. The senator, I'm told, is a tolerable
actor. But heretofore his roles have not been in the
realm of comedy. I thought his opening lines hilarious.

In the name of common decency, Senator, are we
prepared to say that our country has not spent billions
and billions of dollars in all sorts of covert activities,
murder, and mayhem to influence elections and over-
throw governments around the globe? What about
Guatemala, Nicaragua, Chile? What about our power-
brokering in Iran and Iraq, those squandered hours that
continue to bedevil us?

As a mere lad I spent three years in defense of my country. Now at ebb tide, I wish for a level of integrity from it. So why not stick to serious roles, Senator? Leave the comedy to Jay Leno and late-night television.

⟫◆⟪

V

WHEN YOU WRITE RARE BOOKS FOR A LIVING, PAYDAYS ARE SOMETIMES SPORADIC. Some years ago my wife said one of us had to get out and find a real job. I sensed a preference. Waylon Jennings, a neighbor and old friend, gave me the prestigious position of cook on his tour bus. Waylon is not noted for excessive piety, but I learned an important theological lesson from him. Late one night I said, "Waylon, what do you believe?"

"Yeah," he answered. On an overnight stagecoach, a conversation need not be rushed. After a long silence I asked, "Yeah? What's that supposed to mean?" Quiet again, until Waylon said, "Uh-huh." That ended my prying into the state of ole Waylon's soul.

Today we are bombarded with a theology of certitude. I don't find much biblical support for the stance of "God told me and I'm telling you, and if you don't believe as I do, you're doomed." A sort of "My god can whip your god" posture. From Abraham, going out by faith not knowing where he was being sent, to Jesus on the cross, beseeching the Father for a better way, there was always more inquiring faith than conceited certainty.

It occurs to me that the troubadour's response that late night might have been the most profound affirmation of faith I had ever heard. "Yeah. I believe. Don't bother me with all the baggage." Recently he wrote a song about that long-ago conversation. "In my own way I'm a believer," he sings.*

Maybe that's as close as any of us ever get.

*From "I Do Believe" by Waylon Jennings. © Waylon Jennings Music.

⟹◆⟸

VI

GARY GILMORE, IN 1977, WAS THE FIRST PER-
SON TO BE EXECUTED AFTER THE SUPREME
Court ruled it permissible ten years earlier.
Shortly before the state of Utah was to kill him by mus-
ketry, he twice tried to kill himself. And twice the state
went to extraordinary measures to save his life. Somehow that makes no sense to me. If it is in the best in-
terest of society for a man to be dead, what difference
does it make if he does it himself? Unless, of course, we
get some depraved gratification from doing it ourselves.
How then do we differ from the one we kill? Sure, there
are the arguments about guilt and innocence, all based
on Old Testament texts. But the death penalty was pre-
scribed there for twenty-three offenses, including sass-
ing your mamma and having a dangerous ox. All of
them pale into lunacy when viewed in the hot light of
the teachings of Christ.

Now they have killed Carla Faye Tucker in Texas.
Moral leaders from around the world, including the
pope, Billy Graham, and many who support executions
by the state, men such as Jerry Falwell and Pat Robertson, begged that she be spared. We call it the death

penalty. If the Christian doctrine of an afterlife is true, is death really a penalty? I'm not sure what death is. I'm not sure what life is. I do know death is the enemy and life is of God, so we mortals had best be careful how we piddle with it.

I was once asked to debate the death penalty with a well-known scholar. He gave a lengthy and learned statement on why he favored it. I was embarrassed because I had no prepared remarks. So I said, "I just think it's tacky," and sat down. That led to confusion as to just what "tacky" meant. Well, tacky means ugly, no style, no class. I didn't win the debate, but I do believe America as a nation has too much class, too much character, and too much style to go on sinking to the crude level of death practiced in executions. So for the sake of our own soul, let's just cut it out.

⟹◈⟸

VII

THE APOSTLE PAUL, HAVING NO ONLINE WEB SITE, NOT EVEN A TELEPHONE, WROTE A LOT of letters. Several were saved and became part of the Bible. Some of the things he wrote are still highly controversial. Like the idea of total equality of the sexes. There was this upskuttle over in Galatia about that, so he sat down and wrote one of his most famed letters. "Now looka here," he wrote. "In this new movement, there is no such thing as servant or master." ("Neither bond nor free" was the way he put it.) And then the real shocker: "There is neither male nor female."

A lot of us claim to believe everything in the Bible. But neither male nor female? Then how come most of our ministers are men? Some say it's because none of the apostles were women. But none of them were Gentiles either. Others contend it is because males were first in creation, and women were first to fall in the Garden of Eden. But by that logic women would have priority in being ordained. If they discovered sin first, they have been at it longer, and thus should be more adept at identifying sin and casting it out.

Ask your preacher about it. Or maybe bring it up in Sunday school.

VIII

WE REFER TO PEOPLE LIVING ON THE STREET AS HOMELESS. ACTUALLY THEY ARE houseless, not homeless. Their home is wherever they may be. A sad plight, especially with winter coming on.

For the past few weeks, I've been out peddling books. Almost the way people used to do vacuum cleaners and hairbrushes: door to door. In every city I visited I inquired as to the number of people living on the streets. Then I asked how many churches, synagogues, and mosques there were. I was not too surprised to learn that in most cities there are about the same number of houseless people as there are congregations.

Quite often when I make a speech to a church group—they hardly ever ask me to do anything as sacred as a sermon—someone will say, "You complain a lot about the faithlessness of the steeples, but you never tell us what we can do to make the world better."

Well, how about this: Let every congregation adopt one person who lives on the streets. Ask no questions as to the worthiness of these people. Who among us *is* worthy? Just find them lodging, a job, friends—give them hope. That would solve the problem of people living on the streets.

"But how would we afford it?"

"The same way you afford your tall steeples, rich edifices, preachers' salaries, and all the rest. With tithes and offerings."

<hr/>

IX

HEROES COME IN ALL SIZES, COLORS, AND CIRCUMSTANCES. AND RECONCILIATION comes in various ways. I recall a day in 1966 when the elementary school of a small town in Mississippi had a court order to accept black children for the first time. A hate-filled mob had gathered outside, and trouble seemed certain. The school principal approached with a little brown-skinned six-year-old. A burly white man tried to block the way. "There's going to be blood and guts flowing in the streets," he said to the principal. That narrowed the field of contention, for there weren't but three streets in the little town.

"I've seen both," the principal answered. "And I'll be right back." He was a well-built man with a flattop haircut, looking more like a marine drill sergeant than an elementary school administrator.

After he walked the child into the building, he returned. His adversary was gone.

The schoolmaster was also chief of the volunteer fire department. Sometime later the heckler's house was on fire and the schoolman-turned-fireman raced to the scene. Eventually he climbed down from the attic, smelling of smoke and soaked with perspiration. "Your house is secure," he said.

"Do you remember what I said to you that day when you were bringing the colored kids to school?" the man asked.

"Yes, I do," the principal answered. "And do you remember what I replied?"

"I sure do," the man said. "And that's why I was gone when you got back." The two men shook hands, laughed heartily, and parted as neighbors. Reconciled.

X

THERE ARE LIES BEING TOLD ABOUT THE BIBLE AND AMERICA. BY PEOPLE WHO SHOULD know better, and probably do. They pose as the Messiah's evangelists on programs subsidized with tax exemptions and protected by the same First Amendment they frequently denounce. They clothe a blatantly political agenda in pious rhetoric and peddle it as gospel.

They preach that America was founded by right-wing Christians, who espoused the same theology as they do. Who were these people?* How about John Adams, Daniel Webster, or Thomas Jefferson? Won't work. They were Unitarians. What of Benjamin Franklin? A deist. Thomas Payne? A self-avowed atheist. There were no right-wing pietists in the motley crew that shaped America's earliest documents. They weren't trying to establish a Christian nation. Quite the opposite. They were fleeing from entanglement with anybody's religion, for they had seen where governments based on religion led. They had seen the beggary, the bloodletting inhumanity of theocracies, and wanted no part of it. Church was never to be state. State was never to be church.

Shame on those fat-cat false prophets spewing their toxic rhetoric, trying to control every facet of American life with a selective reading of the Bible. That's blasphemy. It's idolatry. The Bible is a book about who God is, not a political handbook. And America was not founded on legislated morality.

———◆———

*See Frosty Troy, "Persecution of Christians in America: Say What?" *Christian Ethics Today*, February 1998, p. 12.

XI

RECENTLY IN SALT LAKE CITY A PASSEL OF SOULS OF MY RELIGIOUS DECLENSION RE-solved that wives should submit graciously to their husbands. I don't recall that being an issue of any gravity in our family. For example, I am totally irre-sponsible with money, so my wife handles that. She gives me pocket cash and I don't complain. (I reckon I'm not a leader!) But she doesn't know about farming, so in the little bovine cul-de-sac we inhabit I decide what variety of seeds to plant, when and where to plant—things like that. It's worked pretty well for this first fifty-three years of marriage.

Even so, I'm glad to see my Baptist brethren—yes, brethren—taking a solid, literal stand on biblical in-terpretation. Maybe next year they will do the same with the passages where Jesus and Isaiah said they had come to proclaim opening the doors of prisons and let-ting all the prisoners go free. That would rescue us from the prison-industrial complex that threatens to bank-rupt us with ever more costly prison construction.

Or they could pass a resolution about Romans 12, where St. Paul tells us to feed our enemies. Since the president, vice president, and Senator Jesse Helms are all Southern Baptists, we'll lift the sanctions on enemies like Cuba, Iraq, and Libya and send them food for their crying babies. We could even quit spending so much time trying to put prayer in the public schools, because Jesus unambiguously taught that when we pray we are to go to a secret place and pray in secret.

So I'm glad to see my brethren taking scripture seriously. I await even more resolutions.

⸻⬦⬦⸻

XII

TWO FELLOWS SHOWED UP HERE A COUPLE OF YEARS AGO. DIDN'T STAY LONG AT FIRST, BUT they kept coming back. One could speak a little English. I gave them some odd jobs and introduced them to neighbors, who did the same. Their main job was with a construction company. Folks said they were illegal aliens. Since my understanding of our kooky sect called radical Christianity brooks no notion of illegal somebody or alien anybody, we became friends.

One day they came with a beautiful rancher-style hat. My size. "For you, Señor Weel." Proof of purchase was inside the box. Ah, the suspicions people have of illegal aliens.

I like hats—from baseball caps to fedoras to pith helmets to Amish felts. But I knew they had paid a week's wages for this hat. My first impulse was to thank them and say I couldn't accept something that had cost the pay for a week of hard work. Then I remembered something about the grace of acceptance. About how for many of us it is more difficult than the grace of giving. Not only that, I mightily admired the color and style and feel of the hat. And I love the Jimenez brothers.

Two fine, handsome, hardworking young gentlemen, who somehow knew that we don't recognize "illegal alien" as a condition of brotherhood. Because I like hats, I'm glad we don't.

———◆———

XIII

I'VE JUST COME FROM ANOTHER NATIONAL CHURCH CONVENTION. THEY ALWAYS TALK ABOUT race, that matter Gunnar Myrdal, fifty years ago, called an "American Dilemma."

Now it seems not a dilemma, but America's preoccupation and clinical fixation. Strange, for in reality race does not exist. It is a sociological concept, not a tangible reality. God created human beings, and we did the rest. What we did as the rest has been a lot. Part of it was even to own one another in a cruel and baneful system called slavery. Now, at the highest levels of religion and government, it is fashionable to apologize for that.

I'm all for apologies. My mamma taught me good manners, and saying, "I'm sorry" fits within the code of civility. However, my mama and common sense also taught me that if I bump my neighbor off the sidewalk and into the path of an eighteen-wheeler, say, "Excuse me," and walk away, I have served him, God, and civility not at all. It is only if I pick him up, get medical attention, and make amends for his loss that I truly express my regret. In church circles that's known as the story of the Good Samaritan. At the governmental level, it's called affirmative action. Better think about that before we apologize.

———≈◆≈———

XIV

WHY ARE REDNECKS THE LAST MINORITY OF DERISION? LEXICONS GIVE THIS DEFinition: "Redneck: One of the poor, white, rural laboring class of the southern United States." Why the slurs and scorn against poor, rural working people? I was born of poor, rural working-class parents and grew up in the middle of the Great Depression. Why is it if someone is uncouth, rude, vulgar, illiberal, and especially if obnoxiously racist, that person is routinely dubbed a "redneck"? That's not what the word means. Being a low-income worker doesn't make one an unregenerate bigot. Sometimes it's quite the opposite. This month a majority of the laboring class in Houston voted to continue affirmative action, while nearly 80 percent of the carriage trade voted to abolish it.

Few of you would call dark-skinned people—well, you know the "n" word and no respectful person uses it. Our nation is made up of people of many ancestries. There are impertinent invectives some use when referring to each lineage. I don't. So please don't insult me by using the "r" word when referring to a dolt. I am of the loins of poor, white, rural laboring people of the South. I'm a redneck, but I'm not a trashy bigot.

XV

THE "EVER-ROLLING STREAM" CALLED TIME IS BOTH COMFORTING AND REPROVING. FIFTY-three years ago, August 6, 1945, I stood with my buddies on a cliff on the island of Saipan. After more than two years overseas, about the only recreation we had was watching the hefty bombers land on nearby Tinian Island. "I'll bet that's the one!" someone screamed. It was the *Enola Gay*, a plane we had seen many times. We had been told by way of an underling grapevine that something big had happened, something so extraordinary that the war would soon end and we would be going home. We knew nothing of the details and didn't care. We were cheering, pretending the cheap PX beer we sprayed on each other was champagne, slapping each other on the back, and throwing steel helmets and M1 rifles into the deep pearly waters of the Pacific Ocean. More than a hundred thousand of God's children lay in carnage—burned, mangled, eviscerated. Dead. And we cheered.

Thirty years later I was part of another vigil. This one outside a Florida prison near where I had trained as a soldier. A single one of God's children was about to die inside the prison. A group of young men and women nearby cheered as lustily as we had done on Saipan that day. "That's it! That's Ole Sparky!" I heard as the lights inside the prison walls blinked from a power surge. "Fry the bastard! Fry the bastard! Bring on the barbecue sauce." Their callous chant was sickening. Then I felt a greater affliction: the sudden realization that I had once celebrated death as crudely as they were doing. How different, then, was I from the odious adolescents of central Florida? But for time. And grace. That bequest that trumps the chants of us all.

———◆———

XVI

A FEW WEEKS AGO I HAPPENED UPON TWO MIDDLE-AGED MEN FIGHTING. NOT A schoolyard scuffle, but a genuine ball-fisted, bloodletting kind of adult jawbreaker. Emergency room stuff. "What's going on here?" I asked a bystander.

"A fight," he shrugged, grinning at my dumb question.

I begged the men to stop. One yelled back for me to mind my own business unless I wanted a beating myself. I didn't, so I chose his first suggestion and drove away.

Another war in the Persian Gulf seemed certain at the time. I thought of that and of the two men fighting. Neither made any sense to me. "But still they have weapons of mass destruction," we are told. Really? We have enough such weapons to kill everyone on earth many times over.

A fistfight is about hurting someone. But war is about killing. Most sadly it is about killing children. That should bother everyone. For certain, our nation has done its share of killing children. From the Trail of Tears to Dresden to Hiroshima to My Lai to Waco. Ah, we have killed children, all right. I believe that taking human life at any age or stage of development is wrong. And please don't tell me that's none of my business.

Why can there not be a one-sentence peace treaty: "It shall be a violation of international law for any nation to kill a child of another nation." What nation would not sign the treaty? And how would war then be waged?

⟻⬦⟼

XVII

ON A WARM MISSISSIPPI EVENING FIFTY-SIX YEARS AGO, MY FATHER, GRANDFATHER, uncle, two neighbors, and a country parson ordained me a Baptist preacher. That's the Baptist way. They said that as a Baptist I was free to think my own thoughts, interpret the scripture on my own, speak my own God-given mind. They called it "soul freedom." I learned that two Baptist preachers, Isaac Backus and John Leland, were responsible for the First Amendment to the Constitution. That means that without the freedom-loving Baptist movement in colonial America, there might never have been an ACLU.

Great folk, we Baptists. Oh, we've made mistakes along the way. Like in 1845 when a passel of us insisted that slavery was the will of God and became *Southern* Baptists. A hundred and fifty-one years later, we apologized. More recently, some of us said that the Disney people were sinful for being charitable to gay and lesbian folk. Someday, mark my word, we'll apologize for that too, recalling that the scripture says that of faith, hope, and charity, charity is the greatest virtue.

In case I'm not around for the apology, I am

exercising now the "soul freedom" my Mississippi kin vested in me so long ago. To celebrate the fifty-six years I've been a Baptist preacher, I am buying some Disney stock for my newborn grandson.

XVIII

USUALLY WHEN I AM INTRODUCED TO SOME-ONE, HE OR SHE WILL ASK, "AND WHAT DO you do, Mr. Campbell?" If I am in a frivolous mode, I sometimes respond, "What do I do about what?"

If a bit more charitable, I might say, "I write rare books. At least, my royalty statements indicate that they are rare." Either the conversation progresses in a civil manner after that, or the person dismisses me as a wisenheimer and returns to his own reverie.

Of course, what that question means is, "What do you do for money? What kind of work do you do?" Not important, I think. Scripture takes a dim view of money. Root of all evil. Jesus even called it filthy. Also, work as it has been known is vanishing in our part of the world. Those who make the really serious money don't work at all. They talk on the phone, go to lunch where they have meetings, talk on the phone some more, and then go to a gym or golf course to do for their body what work used to do. Work, in the sense of physical exer-tion, is rare where making money is involved.

Jesus never asked people what they did for money.

His concern was "How do you justify yourself?" The ultimate inference was, "At the end of a day, or at the end of your life, what have you done to leave the world a little better place than the one you entered?"

⌒⋙⬦⋘⌒

XIX

I'M A CONSERVATIVE. I'M A CONSERVATIVE, AND I'M
GETTING TIRED OF LIBERALS MESSING WITH MY
old-fashioned values. Liberals who masquerade as a
"Christian" coalition. You know, those electronic soul
molesters who hurl to hearth and household their political agenda, all disguised in a tidy and palatable
gospel of "Take up your cross and relax. Take up your
cross and get rich. Take up your cross and send a hurri-
cane scurrying up the coast to blow somebody else's
house to smithereens."

Classic liberalism believed in the "perfectibility of
man," as we said back then. So does the Christian
Coalition. Conservatives took a much dimmer view.
Liberals believed it was the function of big government
to assist in their push to effect change, actually to legislate us into perfection. So does the Christian Coalition.
Conservatives fought such a notion. Conservatives believed that religion, morality, and one's relationship to
God were private matters and that government should
stay out of them. Those liberals I'm talking about want
big government to effect changes that would make our
children pray in public schools and study the Christian

Bible. They want government to require the posting of the Ten Commandments in public offices. They want big government to legislate things like sexual identity and behavior, and which books may be in the libraries.

I'm much too old-fashioned for things like that. I want to hang onto old things. Like the First Amendment to the Constitution. Government, under the kind of theocracy they're lobbying for, will not only be Big Brother, it will be a sort of god. And the First Commandment says, "Thou shalt have no other gods before me." I want old-fashioned values like the First Amendment and First Commandment to be left alone. They have served us well. I don't want big government interfering in my personal life—how I worship or what I read. I want liberals who want the government to control everything to leave us conservatives alone.

In return, I'll leave them alone.

XX

THE PEOPLE IN WASHINGTON THESE DAYS MUST STAY UNCOMMONLY BUSY THINKING OF preposterous things to propose. A recent news item reported Majority Leader Trent Lott talking of legislation to punish China for human rights violations.

A senator from Mississippi? That's where I'm from. Can we, sir, with any moral authority, reprove another for human rights violations? Have we so soon forgotten how we deceived and defeated the primeval inhabitants of our state in dishonorable treaties, bringing about the ignominious Trail of Tears? Our own brand of ethnic cleansing. Do we now ignore the long, dark night of captivity of an entire race and the system that followed which we called sharecropping, but which bordered on peonage? Restriction of the ballot until recent times? Ask your colleague in the other chamber, Congressman John Lewis, about human rights in our state. He will tell you of standing naked for hours in Auschwitz fashion in our penitentiary, guarded by deputies with cattle prods. His crime? He was trying to ride a Greyhound bus as a human. Ask the ghosts of

Fannie Lou Hamer, Medgar Evers, and countless others: the strange fruit that hung from poplar trees, or floated downstream in the Tallahatchie River. The list of our own human rights violations is long, sir. And a man both you and I call "Lord" cautioned us about ranting over the sawdust in the eye of another while ignoring the plank in our own eye.

So. Careful, Senator.

XXI

WHEN YOU LIVE IN THE NASHVILLE AREA, YOU HAVE TO KNOW THREE CHORDS ON a guitar to get a driver's license. We lived too far from town to walk, so I learned my three chords. In the process we became friends with quite a number of our country music neighbors. Tom T. Hall, a songwriter, novelist, and performer, was one of them. Mr. Hall called me the other day and said he had a solution to one of America's most troubling political problems: prayer in the public schools. He is generally a man of unusual wit and wisdom, so I listened. "That fight is tearing this country apart. Educators should be left alone to educate." I agreed. "All right, then. Let's agree that it is quite proper for prayer to be a part of education." I said I couldn't endorse compelled praying. Then he gave me his solution: "Let's make it homework."

We talked on. Those who press most ardently for prayer in the public schools are also champions of family values. And who isn't? So to make school prayer homework is to encourage family values. "The family that prays together stays together" is an old saying. My friend said if teachers can require pupils to do an hour of calculus, or read a certain book for thirty minutes before returning to school next day, surely they can say, "And also spend five minutes with your family in prayer or meditation."

"H'mmm." Muslims could pray to Allah, Jewish families to Yahweh, Christians in Jesus' name. No one's religion is violated. "What about atheists?" I asked.

"Atheists meditate," he answered.

It did seem a simple answer to an ever more divisive problem. But maybe the problem is too prized in political demagoguery to accept such a simple solution.

—————

XXII

I READ IN THE PAPER THAT A CHRISTIAN CON-
GREGATION WAS TAKING SOMEONE TO COURT
for opening a topless bar on its block. The church
said it was against the law for a topless bar to be that
close to the house of the Lord.

I thought of that scripture warning us against suing
one another, and also remembered the sin of self-
righteousness. So this lawsuit confused me. But more
than that. I know what a bar is, all right, but I'm not
sure what a bar without a top would look like, or what
the purpose would be, or why it would be wrong. My
wife said I was not to go there to find out, but she was
pretty sure it had nothing to do with a bar that had no
top on it. She said my confusion probably had to do
with my longevity.

Maybe so, but I was taught as a child that the church
exists to convert sinners and cast out evil. So it seems
to me if a place is sinful, we would want it just as close
to the church door as possible. That way we could get
to know the sinners, perhaps become friends with them,
maybe even love them, and have a better chance of con-
verting them. Then again, maybe my wife is right and
my confusion has to do with my years. Whatever, it's
something to think about.

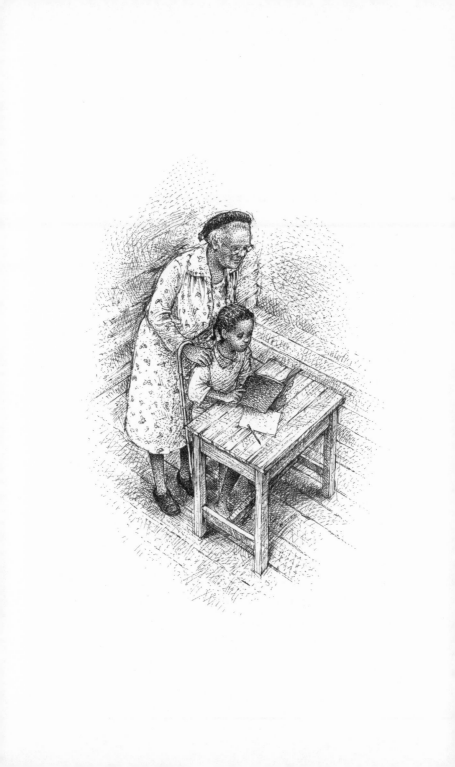

XXIII

I DON'T THINK MUCH OF THE WAY GREATNESS IS GAUGED AND HISTORY IS TAUGHT. IT SEEMS TO center around a few of the rich and famous. Those we call the "little people" seem not to exist. Wars are the generals. Big industries, the CEOs. The body politic, the famed.

My phone rang at the time the networks were trying to decide whether to carry the State of the Union address of the president or the verdict of the O. J. Simpson trial. "Mrs. Booker passed a while ago," my caller said. Two famous people were on TV. I would call my friend back? No, no.

Mrs. Fannye Booker. Ever hear that name? Well, she was a ninety-year-old black lady in Mississippi. She never played football, but she ran a little camp school for rural black children during the Depression, when the state wouldn't educate them. They brought butter, eggs, peas, and cornmeal as tuition. She was never president, but while running a quilting bee she taught black people how to register to vote. She was never a CEO, but she gave hope to hundreds of poor children.

Few came to her funeral. The papers didn't mention

her passing. So let's speak her name now with awe, for she was the stuff of authentic history, the essence of true greatness. Fannye Thomas Booker.

And be grateful.

———⟢◆⟣———

XXIV

THIRTY-TWO YEARS AGO THE HOME OF A BLACK FAMILY IN HATTIESBURG WAS DOUSED with gasoline and set afire. The father, Mr. Vernon Dahmer, stood firing his shotgun through the front door so the family could escape out a back window. Today the children remember being huddled with their father in a nearby barn, his lungs seared from the intense heat, skin peeling from his body like willow bark. He soon died in the arms of his wife.

Recently, the Imperial Wizard of the White Knights of the Ku Klux Klan was tried. The prosecution left little question of guilt. But during the trial, as I visited with both the accused and the Dahmer family, something troubled me. The rationale for another trial, after three hung juries, was that thirty years ago Mississippi was a police state and getting a conviction was impossible. But a police state has higher-ups directing it, not everyday Klansmen. So when will the governors, the rulers, be tried?

"How do you feel?" a journalist asked as the convicted Klansman was led away.

"I feel deep compassion for him," I answered.

"Why?" he asked.

"Because he's a prisoner of the state," I explained. Jesus said nothing about ideology or gravity of offense. We are to be with the prisoners because they are prisoners—be they governors, Klansmen, or innocent victims. That notion began with a sweet child in a manger. It was sealed with a swarthy, sweaty, bloody convict hanging on a cross.

Miss Velma Westbury used to say, "If you just love the folks what's easy to love, that really ain't no love at all." She said, "If you love one, you have to love 'em all." That is the radical message of Easter. That is the glad tidings of Christmas.

Of course, some folks said Miss Velma was crazy.

———⟾◆⟸———

XXV

NOW ABOUT THE NEW MILLENNIUM—IT DOESN'T BOTHER ME MUCH. I'M NOT INTO high finance, I don't fly airplanes, my clock is an old windup Big Ben. They say the "glitch" (whatever that is) may cut my electricity off, but for the first seventeen years of my life, we didn't have electric lights, indoor plumbing, and all that, so I'll survive that little bother. A friend said he is writing a country song about it to the tune of "On Top of Old Smoky." Something about everyone meeting at Mecca on the first day of the new era. He didn't have it all worked out, but it strikes me that would be a good idea. Most of the serious wars today are by people of competing religions. That's absurd. Let's do it this way: Judaism is the oldest of the three major faiths. Christianity is the adolescent in the middle, and Islam is the youngest. The youngest is generally favored in a family. So let's all go to their house, all kneel on a rug and put our heads to the ground, and pray, vowing as we do never to kill one another again in the name of God.

Crazy? Sure, but not quite as crazy as myriad killings over strips of land, bombs planted in embassies, missiles slammed into sites in retaliation, only to start the process all over again. And sooner or later the inevitable. The plan is nowhere near as crazy as the ever-escalating threat of a little country most people never heard of getting hold of the relatively simple technique of making nuclear bombs and in a fit of pique and revenge, and with little to lose, pulverizing the globe.

So, who's crazy? See you at Mecca.

XXVI

A FELLOW MOVED IN OUR AREA SOME WHILE
BACK WHO'S NOT EXACTLY POLISHED
around the fringes. Very bright, owns a big
construction company, and some think he works at
being a rube. Mixes casual dress with high fashion,
chews tobacco, gets often in the grape and uses flawed
grammar on purpose. His name is Pebo. At least, that's
the only call he'll answer. He plays a pretty mean guitar,
and we have a little country band he calls the MF's.
(Our tractors are Massey-Fergusons.) Some evenings
we gather in his equipment shop, and Pebo boils
peanuts, fries catfish, and makes what he calls swamp
gravy, and we pick till midnight.

Pebo has one cultural blemish. He uses the "n" word.
I wish he didn't, but he does. An urbane, proper lady
came by recently and said our families didn't use that
word and Pebo ought to stop it if we are going to be
friends and playmates. I reminded her of the violent
winter storm that swept through our hollow a few years
ago. Roads were blocked and power lines down. While
our families spent the night huddled around their fires,
sipping sour mash and roasting hot dogs, Pebo was on

his bulldozer till daybreak. Clearing the roads, delivering coal, medicine, and food to the poor among our black and white neighbors. She said that didn't excuse his use of the "n" word. I agreed, but reminded her of some words of Jesus: "Not those who say, 'Lord, Lord,' but those who do the will of God." I reckon there's more than one way to use the "n" word, be it verbally or by callous disregard for the neighbor near at hand. There is political correctness, all right. But there is also moral correctness. Deep down, Pebo knows about both. Too many of us, I fear, don't.

⋙◆⋘

XXVII

THIS IS MORE A REMINISCENCE THAN A COMMENTARY. SUCH ARE THE WAYS OF OLD MEN. Little Rock. September, 1957. It was a children's war, really. Nine young children pitted against the political structure of the state, armed troops, and a howling mob. The Supreme Court said they could attend Central High School. Governor Orval Faubus said them nay.

The young children set out from Dunbar Community Center at about ten o'clock to face the soldiers and the hostile crowd. They would be turned back that day, the odds against them too great, their advocates too few. But true to the attributes of the young, they would not forgo their mission. They would be back.

One child, the youngest of the nine, deceptively frail in appearance, was separated from the others. Elizabeth Eckford was her name. As the others approached the warlike phalanx of the soldiers, she was alone. When she made it to a bench near the campus and sat down, exhausted and unsure of what to do, a white man approached and sat down beside her. "Don't let them see you cry," he whispered. But she did cry. Her weeping, though, was not from fear. She cried of a broken heart, a young heart broken by a people who would either commit these atrocities themselves, or do nothing to stop them.

Maybe we learned something that day. Learned enough that we will never again turn away from our weeping children seeking justice.

In the end the children prevailed.

———◆———

XXVIII

I THOUGHT THEY WOULD NEVER FINISH WITH ALL THAT MESS ABOUT MR. CLINTON'S IMPRO-priety in the White House. Never mind the nation and the world's forbidding problems. Even if it left the Constitution repudiated and the republic moldering on the junkheap of failed dominions, partisanship seemed ascendant. Enough.

I was on a flight home. The initials WWJD were engraved on a silver bracelet around my seatmate's wrist. As the plane made its way through the fluffy clouds of early morning, he asked if I knew the Lord. Was I born again? Was I sure? Did I remember the exact day and hour when I had been saved? He did.

Then he turned to a protracted harangue on the presidential controversy, the media wrought Starr Report his sole authority. "Impeachment is an inadequate punishment," he said.

When I inquired, he told me WWJD stood for "What Would Jesus Do?" Clearly our understandings of the radical nature of the Christian faith differed. It was my turn to witness to him, but the cock crew. I didn't do it.

He had told me that he believed in forgiveness, all right, but only if the offending party deserved it, repented, and genuinely apologized. (Deserved it?) I should have told him that in the Christian understanding of grace there are no antecedents. The grace, the forgiveness, is on the part of the one offended, not the offender. No groveling required. And no conjunctions. No "ifs" or "buts." Grace, forgiveness, is not contingent on what the offender does or does not do.

I should have told him there are ten commandments, not one, and that we all violate one or another most every day. I should have pointed to his bracelet, "What Would Jesus Do?" and reminded him that Jesus once confronted a situation analogous to the one Mr. Starr and Congress faced. Jesus ridiculed the accusers of the woman caught in adultery right off the execution yard.

In the end, who was left to cast the first stone in the presidential imbroglio? Would it have been Pat Robertson, so furiously judgmental about the sin of the president? But hadn't Mr. Robertson lied about his own transgression: falsifying the date of his marriage because his premarital sex had resulted in an unwed pregnancy?* Was it Congressman Hyde, whose "youthful indiscretion" at forty lasted five years? What about that alleged murder in the White House, Dr. Falwell? Congressman Burton maybe? Congressman Watts, accused of siring a child out of wedlock and refusing to support him?** Congressman Gingrich? Various senators peering uneasily from behind their own fly-specked masks? You? Me? Just who? Where are the faultless ones? The scripture says there is none righteous. So we sowed the wind, Mr. Starr. And reap the whirlwind.

I should have said all that. Instead, I dozed all the way to Nashville.

*See Paul Taylor, "Robertson Assails 'Outrageous' Reports," *Washington Post*, October 9, 1987, sec. A, p. 1.

**See Frosty Troy, "Persecution of Christians in America: Say What?" *Christian Ethics Today*, February 1998, p. 13.

XXIX

A NEIGHBOR'S HUSBAND LEFT HER RECENTLY. "YOU JUST DON'T MAKE ME HAPPY," HE TOLD her. I have no idea what that means. Happiness is a deceptive, illusory, and elusive thing. Happiness is a fugitive one never finds by pursuing. It seems to be a matter of grace, and generally is not contingent on the behavior of another.

"You're just not what?" "Just not happy." I have been present at several hundred weddings in my day. Never has the officiant exacted a plight that one party will make the other happy. For better or worse. In sickness and health. To love and to cherish. But nothing about happiness. That is simply not a part of the contract.

We don't live in a happy age—not if by happy we mean animated, chuckling, rhapsodic good times. My parents were of the yeomanry. When they married at seventeen and nineteen, it was for a helpmate. Both worked the fields of a small cotton farm in the midst of the Great Depression. We children, three boys and a girl, worked alongside them. The weeds were high, the summer days long and hot. I do not recall the word "happy" ever being used. If it came, we had neither lusted after it nor did we give it a name. It was not in the credit line. We found meaning and purpose in the reality of our existence and dependence on one another. Better perhaps for the word not to be in the lexicon at all. For too frequently "happiness" is an evasion of our real problem. Or an alibi for our frailty.

———◆———

XXX

IT WAS DECEMBER 1943, AND WE WERE ON A CROWDED TROOPSHIP BOUND FOR THE SOUTH Pacific. Most of us were in our teens—seasick, homesick, and a little afraid.

I had asked my best pal, Herman Hyman, what he was going to send his girlfriend for Christmas. "Nothing," he answered. Seemed strange. He mumbled something about Hanukkah, and changed the subject. I had no idea what he meant. I was a naive little Baptist boy from rural Mississippi. Herman was from the Bronx.

What had promised to be a bleak Christmas turned even more dreary when the KP list was read over the ship's intercom. I was to be on kitchen duty on Christmas Day. The sergeant told us we would be crossing the international date line, so there would be two December 25ths.

"I'll do it for you," Herman said.

"Why?"

"Because I want to," he laughed, patting me on the head like a mascot. Herman was older than I.

At the end of the second Christmas in a row, Herman found me alone on the stern of the ship, looking back at where we'd been. He looked very tired. He handed me a can of ripe olives he had lifted from the officers' mess. "Merry Christmas," he said, with a feigned and fatigued "Ho-ho-ho."

"Why'd you do that?" I asked. Over and over.

He sighed in a sort of, You really don't know, do you? fashion. Then he answered, "Because I'm a Jew, little buddy. And Jews don't celebrate Christmas." He told me all about Hanukkah: about another war that was fought two hundred years before my Jesus was even born; about how the Maccabees whipped the Syrians, and the big celebration and rededication of the Temple in Jerusalem. He said we would have a big celebration one day. He told me about how his father would light a candle every night for eight nights, about the good food his mother prepared, and he named all the kinfolk who gathered.

There weren't any Jews in my little rural community—no Catholics, Methodists, or Presbyterians either. Just Baptists. But there was a Jew there when I got back. Herman Hyman died for his country in the last days of the Battle of Saipan. When the war was over and I went home to Mississippi, Herman went with me.

Happy Hanukkah, Herman. You would be seventy-six now. I'll light the eighth candle and we'll be together again. And tell Father Abraham it's my time for KP.

⟹◆⟸

ABOUT THE AUTHOR . . .

WILL DAVIS CAMPBELL IS A WRITER, PREACHER, FARMER, AND SOCIAL ACTIVIST. A NATIVE of Mississippi and a graduate of both Wake Forest University and Yale Divinity School, Will served in the South Pacific in World War II, as a university chaplain, and during the 1950s and '60s, Campbell was among the most conspicuous white Southerners for social justice in the civil rights movement.

He is the author of *Brother to a Dragonfly*, a finalist for the National Book Award, named by *Time* magazine as one of the ten most notable works of nonfiction of the 1970s, and winner of both the Christopher Award and the Lillian Smith Book Award. His very first book, *Race and the Renewal of the Church*, was published by Westminster Press in 1962. *Soul Among Lions: Musings of a Bootleg Preacher* is his seventeenth book.